THE HORNS AND HOOVES OF THE GOAT:

A History of Istria and its People

by Robert Mansuri

Dorrance Publishing Co
585 Alpha Drive
Suite 103
Pittsburgh, PA 15238
Visit our website at *www.dorrancebookstore.com*

ISBN: 979-8-8852-7186-8
eISBN: 979-8-8852-7642-9

The Horns and Hooves of the Goat:

A History of Istria and its People

Bibliography

Lists of sources

The Celtics by Gerhard Herm
Pub. St Martiors Press
A History of Croatia by Stephen Gazi
Pub: Barnes and Nobles INC.
The Early Medieval Balkans
By John V.A Fine, Jr.
The University of Michigan Press
"Croatia" by Dubanko Houatic
A Nervous Splendor by Frederick Morton
The Downtown Tampa Hillsborough
County Public Library-Main Branch.

Dedicated to my Istrian grandparents,
Ivona and Anton,

and my Istrian American mother, Carmen.

SECTION I

ORIGINS OF ISTRIA

After the Thera volcano erupted on the isle of Santorini in 1220 B.C.E., the Illyrians came to Istria. There were three main Illyrian tribes, the Liburnians, Delmates, and Ardiaces. They came to Istria and Croatia during the Iron Age from the Unetice culture which took its name from a village near Prague, Czech Rep. The Unetice culture was an early Bronze Age culture which was the mother culture of the following peoples: Teutons, Umbrians (Central Italy), the Illyrians (Istria and Croatia), Phrygians and Proto-Armenians (Anatolia).

In 391 B.C.E., the Celtic tribes defeated the Romans and conquered Istria. The Celts left their genetic imprint as well as their cultural influence on Istria with the introduction of the Vela Supela (Bag Pipes) and the Prebirat (a folk dance similar to the Irish Jig). The Celtic people also left a culinary influence on Istria with the dish of cabbage, pork, and potato, which is still served in Istria today.

The Romans conquered all of Istria which they called the province of Illyricum and the major port city of Albona (Labin) IN 177 B.C.E. The Roman Emperor Diocletianus (284-6CE) brought the forefathers of all Slavic peoples to Istria and Dalmatia. These people were called Sarmatians and were brought to Istria and Dalmatia as Roman slaves. The term, slave, was derived from Slav. The Sarmatians' original homeland was located between the Vistula and Volga rivers in what is now the Baltic states, eastern Poland and western Russia. After the fourth century B.C.E., the Sarmatians were driven out of their homeland by the Hunnic invasions across the Carpathian mountains and along the Danube.

In 375 C.E., the Goths conquered the Slavs. Then in 493 C.E., the Ostrogoth Theodoric set up a kingdom which included Istria. In the sixth century C.E., the Croatians, with mixed Slavic and Iranian ancestry came to Istria and what would become modern Croatia. In 614C.E., the Avars, a barbarian tribe, sacked Salona, the capital of Istria and Dalmatia.

In 626 C.E., the Avars were defeated at Constantinople by the Byzantine empire. In 670 C.E., the Bulgarians crossed the Danube and set up a state. The Croatians fell under the influence of the Bulgarians in the east and the Franks in the west. The Franks conquered Istria in the second half of the eighth century C.E. Frankish influence was short-lived in Istria however. By the ninth century C.E., the Croatians set up their own duke and fought a series of wars with Venice from 800-910 C.E. In 800 C.E., Viseslav became the first Croatian duke of the Christian faith. Venice invades Istria and sets up Italian schools. In 865C.E., Venice begins a war with Croatia. In 876 C.E., Croatian duke Domagoj tries and fails to liberate Istria from the Venetians. In 877 C.E., Venice is finally forced to sign a peace treaty with Croatia.

In 910 C.E., Tomaslav becomes king of Croatia, Dalmatia, and Istria. He unites Croatia, with his seat of power in Tomaslav Grad in Bosnia, he also defeats the Hungarians. The Bulgarian king Simeon attacks Croatia in 926 C.E. and is badly defeated in Bosnia by Tomaslav. Tomaslav dies in 928C.E. In 1058C.E., Peter Kresimir becomes king of Croatia and Dalmatia. Kresimir built the town of

Sibenik in 1066 C.E. He also chose Roman Catholicism over Eastern Orthodoxy.

In 1102 C.E., the Croatian tribes united with King Koloman of Hungary in Biograd. From 1102-1301C.E., Croatia was ruled by the Arpad Royal family of Hungary. In 1241-2C.E., the Mongols defeated a Croat-Hungarian army in Hungary. The Mongols were defeated at sea at the battle of Pag and finally were defeated in Istria at Grobnicko Polje, a valley in the interior of Rijeka. From 1358 -1526 Croatia lived under Hungarian rule. It was during this time that the Vlachs, a people related to Romanians, moved into first Croatia in the 14th century and into Istria in the 15th century. They were also known as Morlachs or Cici and later most converted to Islam. From 1527 whop on Jan. 1 Habsburg Emperor Ferdinand of Austria took Istria to 1918, Istria was ruled by the Habsburg dynasty.

SECTION III
MODERN ISTRIA

From 1527-1918, when Karl I abdicates, Istria is under the Habsburg Empire. In 1914, WWI breaks out and Italy fights Austria for control of Istria. The Italians and Austrians fight on the Karst of Istria. Italy fights with the Allies in WWI and agrees to fight against Austria but not against Germany. The reason for this is to acquire Istria from Austria as the spoils of war. This did, in fact, happen with the Allied victory over the Central powers of Austria and Germany. The period between WWI and WWII, which was from 1918 to 1945, was a time of Italian repression of Istria. Mussolini and the Italian government wanted to eradicate non-Italian influences in Istria. In 1926 the Italian government banned Slav languages and many South Slav traditions. Italy also wanted to colonize Istria with South Italy's poor. The simmering hatred among the newcomers and the indigenous Slav population would boil over during WWII.

In 1945, Tito's (Josef Broz's) partian forces occupy Istria and begin to execute pro- Fascists by both throwing them off Istrian cliffs and throwing Italian sympathizers into what were called foibes (pits or wells). The pro-Fascists were called Ustaches under a man named Ante Pavelich, who was born in a hut in Bosnia. This was ironic because the pro-Hitler Pavelich's wife was a Jew. The Ustaches lose the war.

From 1945-1991, Tito rules Istria as part of an artificial Yugoslavia or land of the south Slavs. In 1991 Croatia declares its independence from Yugoslavia and civil war breaks out. Istria is cut in two; the northern part becomes part of Slovenia, and the rest is part of Croatia. The flag of Istria, which is a yellow goat with horns, becomes part of the Croatian crest. The schools from 1945-Present are Slavic and Italian is no longer taught. There are Istrian independence parties and they formed the DDI (Istrian DEMOCRATIC DIET) in 1990 before the break-up of Yugoslavia. Croatia and Slovenia are both united in opposing Istrian independence. In 1993, the Croatian Istrians rejected Croat nationalism when the DDI got 72% of the vote.

Section IV
Religion of Istria

The Illyrians practiced the Roman religion until the arrival of the Croatians in the sixth century C.E. The ancient religion of the Croatians was Zoasterianism and later Manichanism. In the seventh, century C.E., the first converts (to Catholicism were made in Istria and Dalmatia. In 680 C.E., there was an understanding reached between the Papacy and the croatian chieftains. Istria was mostly Catholic from the seventh century onwards up to the present. There were two exceptions to this rule in Istria and Bosnia. Bosnia and Istria were part of Croatia proper.

In Bosnia, there developed a hybrid form of Christianity which was called the Bogomil church. It was a combination of the old croatian religion of Zoasterianism and Christianity. It was considered heresy by the Catholic church. The Bogomils later converted to Islam when the Ottomans took over Bosnia. There were people in Istria who were called Morlachs or Vlachs or even Cici. These people were followers of Islam and came in the 15th century. There survives in the Istrian language the word "Vlachi." This word is derogatory and means boorish peasant.

In regards to Catholicism, the Croatian king Tomaslav holds two religious councils, one in 925C.E. and the other in 928 C.E. In these councils, Tomaslav gives the Bishop of Split

jurisdiction over Istria. In the 1050's, there is a conflict over whether to use Latin or the old Glagolitic script at mass. In 1060, it is decided that Latin must be used. Under the Habsburg rule, Istria was mostly Catholic because the Austro-Hungarian empire was predominantly Catholic. It continued to be Catholic between WWI and WWII under Italy. After WWII, Istria was under Yugoslavia and Tito, and the government discouraged religion and the people were Atheist. Since 1991, when Yugoslavia broke up, Croatia ruled and religion made a comeback. The war after Yugoslavia broke up firmly ingrained the different ethnicities and religions of the region.

Section V
Language of Istria

In the beginning, the people of Istria spoke an Illyrian language related to and similar to modern Albanian and Romanian. When Istria became part of the Roman empire, people spoke Latin. When the Croatians came to Istria, they brought their Slavic language, but people still used Latin in their liturgy and they used the Roman alphabet, not the Cyrillic. The Venetians came to Istria in the 800's C.E. and set up Italian schools. From 1527-1918, under Habsburg rule, there were both Italian and Slavic schools in Istria.

After 1918, Italy took control of Istria. The Italians passed laws in 1926 banning the Slavic language and the South Slav traditions of the Istrian people. It is worthy of noting that although Habsburg Emperor Franz Joseph in 1889 made German the language of the Austrian armed forces, the emperor never banned any language of the empire. From the time of Austrian rule, the people of Istria had their own main dialect that had both elements of the Italian and Slavic languages which was called "Ponase," meaning "our way." It is basically a Slavic dialect with Italian components The Italian words in Ponase are similar to the Venetian and Triestine dialects. During the Italian rule, there were only Italian schools.

From 1945-1991, Istria was ruled by Tito and Yugoslavia. Tito built only Slavic schools and they taught only Serbo-Croatian in the Cyrillic alphabet. Ponase continued to be spoken. In 1991, Croatia took over Istria and reintroduced the Roman alphabet. There was conflict over the alphabet when Yugoslavia broke up. There was even a Serb who was killed for writing "Long Live Serbia" in the Roman, not the Cyrillic alphabet. Language continues to be a bone of contention in the region.

Section VI
Food of Istria

When Istrians came to America, their two main professions were chefs and seamen. Istrian food has many different influences The food is a combination of Slavic, Celtic, Austro-Hungarian and Italian cuisine. The examples of Istrian culinary excellence are varied and many. Istrians made a northern Italian dish called Polenta, which is simply boiled or fried corn meal. Another Italian dish is Gnocchi, which are potato dumplings and can be served with various ragouts and sauces. Yota is another culinary delight, which is a Hungarian soup made of sauerkraut, pork, potato, and red kidney beans. Palacinke are Hungarian crepes filled with sugar or jam. Putica is a Croatian holiday bread made of nuts and chocolate. Boiled beef which is Austrian. Bacon, cabbage, and potato is Celtic in origin. Krafi is a polish dumpling stuffed with raisins. Strudel is from the Austrian rule. There are two dishes which are native to Istria: Pasutice, which is a pasta dough usually served with salted sardines, breadcrumbs, and olive oil, and Fuzi, which is a light pasta. Finally, there are two dishes, which go together, which are served on Christmas Eve and Good

Friday. These are Bacccala, which is cod fish, which is beaten with olive oil and garlic, and a soup made with garlic, olive oil, chick peas, white beans, and pasta.

Section VII
Conclusion

The Istrian people have had numerous and varied influences from diverse countries, empires, and cultures on their history, religion, language, cuisine, and culture. The people of Istria have the genetic imprints of the Romans, Celts, Austrians, and most importantly the Slavic people. Istria has been an important seaport for the landlocked Austro-Hungarian empire as well as the birthplace of the Roman emperors Constantine and Diocletianus. Istria has never had a separate independent state of its own. It has a unique cultural identity but is a nation without a state. It remains to be seen if the region will ever have a national independent state. For now, it is content to be ruled by the major ethnic group in Istria, the Croatians. Istria shares religious and ethnic ties with Croatia; therefore, it should be proud that its goat coat of arms is incorporated in the Croatian crest. Since the 10th century, when Istria was under Tomislav, all or part of Istria has been under Croatian rule so it is only natural that Istrians should be united with their Croat brothers.